A-22332

500.5   Branley, Franklyn
BRA   M.

        Mysteries of outer
        space

    $11.95

DATE			
DEC 17 '90			
MAR 19 91			
SM			
FE 0 9 '99			

MYSTERIES OF OUTER SPACE

ALSO BY FRANKLYN M. BRANLEY

MYSTERIES OF THE UNIVERSE SERIES

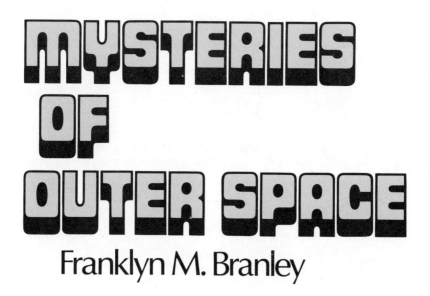

MYSTERIES OF OUTER SPACE

Franklyn M. Branley

Diagrams by Sally J. Bensusen

LODESTAR BOOKS   E. P. DUTTON   NEW YORK

LIBRARY OF CONGRESS CATALOGING IN PUBLICATION DATA

Branley, Franklyn Mansfield, date
  Mysteries of outer space.

  (Mysteries of the universe series)
  "Lodestar books."
  Bibliography: p.
  Includes index.
  Summary: Discusses kinds of space, the sky in outer
space, time in outer space, weightlessness, survival in
space, uses of space, mining the asteroids, and the end
of space.
  1. Outer space—Juvenile literature. [1. Outer
space] I. Bensusen, Sally J., ill. II. Title.
III. Series: Branley, Franklyn Mansfield, date.
Mysteries of the universe series.
QB500.22.B7 1984 500.5 84-13683
ISBN 0-525-67149-8

Published in the United States by E. P. Dutton,
2 Park Avenue, New York, N.Y. 10016

Published simultaneously in Canada by
Fitzhenry & Whiteside Limited, Toronto

Editor: Virginia Buckley   Designer: Riki Levinson

Printed in the U.S.A.   W
10 9 8 7 6 5 4 3

Photograph on opposite page
courtesy of Palomar Observatories

CONTENTS

MYSTERIES OF OUTER SPACE

1 KINDS OF SPACE

What is space?

Most people know very little about space. They would probably say that space is the entire region outside of Earth. And they would be partly right, except that there are many kinds of space—the region beyond Earth is not all the same. Also, many people would say that space means emptiness. They would be right again, but not completely. Compared to our atmosphere, space seems empty. But actually space is far from vacant.

There is probably no region of the universe that is absolutely empty. A cup of Earth's atmosphere contains billions of molecules, while only a single molecule might be contained in many, many cups of outer space. Still, that one molecule would exist. Although matter may be spread very thinly in space, there is still something in space between planets, stars, and galaxies.

Some areas of space contain many more molecules than other regions. Shuttle orbiters may go only two or three hundred kilometers above Earth's surface, but they are in space. They are in terrestrial space just beyond our atmosphere. It is space close to Earth, where there are still a good many molecules.

Farther out, the region around the Moon, is lunar space. And between terrestrial and lunar space is cislunar space (*cis* means this side of).

Beyond the Moon is the space between the planets—interplanetary space. And each planet has its own particular space, such as Martian space or Saturnian space.

Beyond the solar system are the stars. The regions between them make interstellar space.

Stars together make a galaxy. The stars that we see, and many more that we cannot see, make the Milky Way galaxy, an array of some 200 billion stars. The region between galaxies is intergalactic space.

So there are many different kinds of space. A person is bound to wonder where one begins and another ends. There is no sharp division between the various kinds of space. However, certain conditions often exist that enable us to define an area of space as terrestrial, lunar, or something else.

What is the boundary of terrestrial space?

Airplanes must be in air in order to fly. One might say that terrestrial space begins where air no longer supports the flight of airplanes. A better way of explaining this, and the explanation usually given, is to say that terrestrial space begins where spaceships become free of friction with Earth's atmosphere.

The air envelope surrounding Earth extends several thousand kilometers beyond the surface. However, as altitude increases and density of the atmosphere drops off rapidly, the molecules become separated. At about 200 kilometers, the molecules are so thinly spread that they cause very little friction with a vehicle such as an orbiter. The ship moves freely and is not heated by friction at this distance. As you may know, the ship becomes very hot when it comes back through the denser atmosphere when making a landing approach.

Airplanes such as this Boeing 767 do not reach outer space. They need an atmosphere in order to fly.   BOEING PHOTO

Space shuttles fly in terrestrial space. This view of the Challenger was taken from the temporarily free-flying shuttle pallet satellite.   NASA

What is a gravity well?

Frictional heating and drag (the slowing effect of an atmosphere) disappear when the ship reaches terrestrial space. But it is still pulled by Earth's gravity. In fact, gravity of Earth or any other mass extends into space forever.

When a ship goes to the Moon, it must work against Earth's gravity most of the way. You might think of the vehicle as climbing out of a deep well—a gravity well. The well has long, sloping sides that extend almost to the Moon. Once the ship is nearly out of the well, it enters another one—the gravity well of the Moon. At the region that separates the Earth well from the Moon well, an object could fall in either direction. Power or momentum (velocity) is needed to push a ship from one well into the other.

While the moonship is in transit, it is also in the Sun's gravitational field. This field is so powerful that it can hold in orbit even the outermost planets—those that are billions of kilometers away.

The Sun's gravity well is the deepest one in the solar system, and the most far reaching. Along its walls are the wells of each of the planets. And along the walls of many of the planetary wells are the separate wells of each of the planets' satellites.

Gravitation extends throughout space. Wherever there is mass, there is also gravity. The greater the mass, the greater the gravitation. The force drops off with distance, but it never disappears completely. It never becomes zero.

What is the zodiacal light?

Space between planets contains dust and particles. The particles tend to congregate about the more massive planets, such as Jupiter and Saturn, because of the greater gravitation of these planets. However, Earth has enough mass to hold a vast cloud of the particles. Each day billions of them rain down on our

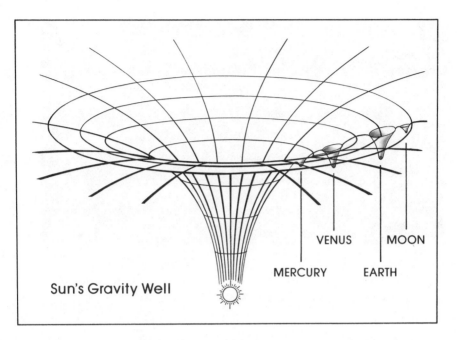

VENUS　　MOON

MERCURY　　EARTH

Sun's Gravity Well

The Sun's gravity well is the deepest one in the solar system.
Along its walls are the less powerful wells of each of the planets.

planet, pulled in by Earth's gravitation. Some people estimate that 20 000 tons of debris fall to Earth each day.

That seems like a tremendous amount, and it is. But when compared to Earth's mass, it is very small indeed. The mass of Earth is 6 sextillion (6×10^{21}) tons. In a hundred years, 20 000 tons a day adds up to only a few millionths of 1 percent of Earth's mass, an amount so small it is hardly worth mentioning.

The dust surrounding Earth is illuminated by the Sun. Right after sunset when the sky is clear, the glow can often be seen in the western sky. It is a cone-shaped formation that extends into space. It has been called the zodiacal light because it lines up with the zodiac, the belt of constellations through which the Sun moves as the year goes by.

Space dust along the Sun's path is lighted by the Sun. Occasionally, the dust can be seen as a soft glow in the western skies shortly after sunset—the zodiacal light.

Where does space dust come from?

Much of the dust is the remains of the big bang, an explosion which many scientists think originated the universe, and planet formation that occurred much later. A good deal of interplanetary dust also comes from comets. It is believed that a cloud of dust lies out beyond the solar system and extends around it. This cloud is the spawning ground of comets. Comets are collections of dust and ice that form inside the comet cloud. A few particles join together, making a cluster that pulls in additional particles, and so the mass grows. At some point, a nearby star, or a planet such as Jupiter, pulls a cluster out of the cloud. That cluster may go into an orbit that takes it around the Sun. The mass of particles has become a comet.

Since the comet core is mostly dust and ice, it is not held together tightly. As the comet nears the Sun, solar gravitation pulls away some of the material that makes the comet, and

As comets pass by the Sun, they lose dust and gases that are ▶ *pulled away by the Sun's gravitation. In this photo of Halley's comet 1910, Venus is visible at top right.* LOWELL OBSERVATORY

PHOTOGRAPH

the matter becomes spread throughout interplanetary space. Planets pass through the dust. Fairly large particles become white-hot as they pass through Earth's atmosphere and the atmospheres of other planets as well. They produce showers of meteors—lights that speed across the sky. Smaller particles that may not produce light also enter our atmosphere. Unnoticed, they rain down onto the surface.

How does space dust affect starlight?

Space dust has not seriously affected our learning about the planets. But it is a factor that astronomers must consider when they study the more distant stars.

Suppose you are looking through dust-laden air at a nearby tree. The amount of dust between you and the tree is small. Therefore the tree appears much the same as it does when the air is clear. On the other hand, suppose you are looking through the same dust at a mountain miles away. Because of the miles and miles of dust, it's possible that the mountain wouldn't even be visible.

And so it is with the stars. When we observe planets, we are looking through many million or a few billion kilometers of dust. The amount of dust is millions of times greater when we focus on the stars. The farthest that Pluto can be from us is about 6 billion kilometers. But the closest star is some 40 trillion kilometers away. Most stars are even farther. And there is dust between them. There isn't much, but when the depth of the dust is trillions of kilometers, it's enough to make a difference in the way a star appears.

Dust causes reddening of starlight, because the dust scatters the blue wavelengths. The longer-wave red light is not scattered, so it comes through to us. This makes stars appear redder than they would if there were no dust in the space that separates us from them. The more distant the star, the redder—and dimmer—it appears to be.

In the 1920s, when astronomers were working out the solution to another mystery (that of the Sun's position in the galaxy), they did not know about interstellar dust and its effect on starlight. Therefore, those early investigators believed the galaxy was much larger than it actually is. They thought it was 300 000 light-years across, partly because distant stars were very dim. (A light-year, in case you don't remember, is the distance that light travels in a year; that's about 10 trillion kilometers.) However, part of that dimness was caused by dust between the stars. When that effect is accounted for, the distance across the galaxy turns out to be more nearly 100 000 light-years.

Is there life in space?

Huge clouds of molecules have been detected in various parts of space. Some are several light-years in diameter. On the average, the mass of these clouds is a thousand times the mass of the Sun. In some of them, density is as high as a million molecules in a cubic centimeter (1×10^6). That's very high for space, although it is very low in terms of Earth's atmosphere, where density is millions of times greater (1×10^{18}).

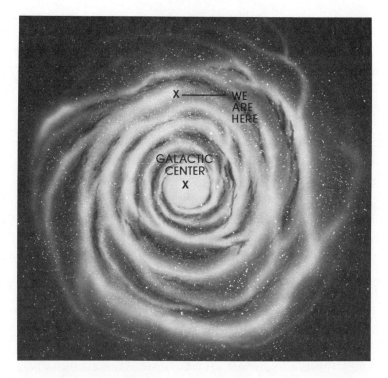

We are located 30 000 light-years from the center of our galaxy, the Milky Way. It is a formation 100 000 light-years across; it contains perhaps 200 billion stars.

Molecules, as you probably know, are made of atoms. For example, a molecule of hydrogen contains two hydrogen atoms; a molecule of water contains two atoms of hydrogen and one of oxygen.

For the most part, the gaseous clouds are made of hydrogen molecules. This leads some astronomers to believe that the clouds are related to the formation of new stars. In addition, small amounts of over fifty different kinds of molecules have been identified in the clouds. Many of the molecules are familiar—alcohol, water, carbon monoxide, and sulfur dioxide. A good many of them are organic, meaning that carbon is part of their composition.

Methane and ammonia are also among the molecules that have been identified. The presence of these two materials is encouraging to those people who believe that life exists out beyond our planet. In an experiment performed several years ago, scientists put methane, ammonia, hydrogen, and water into a container. An electric current was passed through the mixture. After considerable time, the substances had combined to produce amino acids. Proteins are made from these acids. And proteins are the basic molecules of living organisms.

Lightning is an electrical discharge. So, it is reasoned, if those molecules exist where lightning might energize them, it is possible that amino acids would be created. And perhaps those amino acids might in some way become proteins. It would then seem reasonable to suppose that living organisms could emerge.

Lightning is a common condition in the atmospheres of planets. Also, stars explode, and when they do, tremendous amounts of energy are released. Amino acids may be produced throughout interstellar space. When conditions are favorable, those amino acids may become consolidated into proteins. Since the raw materials for proteins exist out among the stars, and since tremendous amounts of energy are released from time to time, some scientists believe that life of some kind may abound in interstellar space.

They may be right. Certainly their reasoning is sound enough for people to give them attention. Whether or not they are correct is the basis for the major mystery of space: Is there life out there?

Is intergalactic space empty?

Our Milky Way galaxy is medium-sized. It is only one of billions of galaxies. Those closest to us are called the Magellanic Clouds. They are about 200 000 light-years away. Another that is fairly near is the Andromeda galaxy, which is 2 000 000 light-years from us. You cannot see the Magellanic Clouds unless

Clouds of gases in our galaxy—such as the Omega Nebula in Sagittarius—contain tremendous amounts of material, some basic to the formation of life.   PALOMAR OBSERVATORIES PHOTO-GRAPH

There are billions of galaxies. This spiral galaxy, photographed edge on, can be seen when looking in the direction of the constellation of Virgo.   PALOMAR OBSERVATORIES PHOTOGRAPH

you are in the southern hemisphere. But the Andromeda galaxy can be seen in the autumn skies. It is in the constellation Andromeda, which is just to the left of the square of Pegasus, the flying horse. Directions for finding it are given in the illustration on page 59. It appears as a dim, fuzzy patch, yet you are looking at billions of stars. If you cannot see the patch, scan the area with binoculars.

There are about twenty galaxies within 2 000 000 light-years of us. They form what is called the local group of galaxies. Other galaxies are far more distant; some of them are billions of light-years away. Space is between them.

It is not empty space. No doubt hydrogen atoms, as well as hydrogen molecules, exist there. And occasionally there may be

Our galaxy belongs to a local group of some twenty galaxies that are located within 2 000 000 light-years of us.

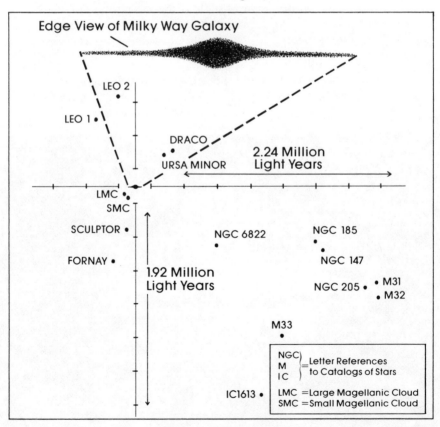

Edge View of Milky Way Galaxy

LEO 2

LEO 1

DRACO

URSA MINOR

2.24 Million Light Years

LMC

SMC

SCULPTOR

NGC 6822

NGC 185

FORNAY

NGC 147

1.92 Million Light Years

NGC 205 • M31
• M32

M33

NGC
M
IC
} = Letter References to Catalogs of Stars

LMC = Large Magellanic Cloud
SMC = Small Magellanic Cloud

IC1613

other molecules, such as those that are found in interstellar space, though one would not expect to find them in abundance. Also, many suspect there may be individual stars, as well as clusters of stars, in the space between galaxies. But there have been no positive identifications of either.

It appears unlikely that there is space dust between galaxies. If there were, the dust would cause reddening of galactic light. You recall that reddening does occur in interstellar space. It is believed that no reddening caused by dust-scattering has been detected in intergalactic space.

Most likely the material between galaxies is largely comprised of ionized hydrogen (a hydrogen ion is an atom from which the electron has been stripped away, leaving the core, the proton). It may be the same material that was formed some 15 billion years ago when the present universe came into existence.

Even though there is a lot of matter in space—between the planets, stars, and galaxies—there is not nearly enough to keep the universe from expanding. It began expanding billions of years ago at the moment of the big bang and has been doing so ever since. The mass of the entire universe, all the matter in it, is not enough to exert sufficient gravitation to pull the universe together. Presently, all parts are moving away from all other parts, and space itself is growing larger. It appears that this expansion will continue forever.

THE SKY IN OUTER SPACE

Are there colors in space?

Here on Earth, daytime is the period when the atmosphere is lighted; sunlight is reflected from water droplets and large molecules in the air. The sky may be dull and gray, deep blue, or have shades of red and many other colors as at sunrise and sunset. During night the sky is black. The nighttime side of Earth is shaded from the Sun.

From a spaceship, the sky is always black. Stars are bright, but the sky itself is dark and colorless. It's the same on Mercury, Pluto, and the Moon, which also don't have atmospheres. Even when the area around a Moon explorer is brightly lighted by the Sun, the sky above is black.

It's black because there is nothing to reflect light. There are no water droplets or large molecules; there is no air. The only things we see are those that reflect light and those that produce light. Right now, the room where you're sitting is filled with light, yet you cannot see the light. You see only those things that reflect light or a lamp that produces light. Outdoors, the space between you and a tree contains light, yet you see only the tree and other objects around it. Light waves are reflected

The Moon has no atmosphere to reflect sunlight, so its sky is black. Shadows, like those cast by this huge split boulder during Astronaut Harrison Schmitt's Apollo 17 moon walk, are deep and cold.   NASA

from the tree. When the light strikes the retinas of our eyes, our brains change the invisible energy into images, and we have vision. We see light reflectors—trees, books, furniture; also light producers—the Sun, a flame, stars, a light bulb. We see light producers only when we look at them directly. (Never look directly at the Sun, for the light is so intense it could damage your eyes.)

Molecules in the sky reflect light. That's why the sky is lighted during daytime hours. If Earth had no atmosphere, our sky would be forever black.

Space is black because there are not enough molecules, or large enough molecules, to reflect the light of the Sun. The Moon's sky is black, as well as the skies of Mercury and Pluto, because there is nothing around them to reflect sunlight. On the Moon you are either in intense sunlight, or deepest darkness. There is no air to spread sunlight, and so soften it.

When astronauts walked on the flat plains of the Moon, they found that a single step or two, such as moving behind a boulder, might take them from bright light into utter darkness. In many places the change was not so great because boulders and hills reflected light into the shadows. Astronauts also experienced dramatic changes in temperature. When they moved into shadows, the thermometer dropped as much as 100° Celsius (C).

Astronauts report that the view from space is fantastic. But that is only when they look back at Earth. Otherwise the scene is monotonous. Except for the stars, which are intensely bright, the sky is black. There is no blue sky or white clouds. Space is black.

How does atmosphere control heat?

On Earth we do not experience such rapid extremes of light or temperature because our atmosphere is like a protective blanket. It reflects light and so softens shadows. Also, objects all about us reflect light and this, too, fills in shadows. In daytime the atmosphere filters sunlight, so we don't get too hot. In the atmosphere there's a layer of ozone that removes much of the ultraviolet light, which is harmful in large amounts.

At night our atmosphere slows the escape of heat. The temperature of the planet holds at close to 14° C. Mercury and the Moon lack atmospheres, so temperatures in those places go very high in the daytime, and they drop very low at night. The range of Mercury is from 350° C to minus 185°. During daytime the Moon temperature reaches 132° and drops to minus 156° at night. Pluto is always cold because it's so far from the Sun.

Objects in space are either brightly lighted or they are absolutely black. Also, they are very hot or very cold. This includes satellites and spaceships. If the vehicles are close to Earth, the shadowed sides pick up light reflected from Earth's clouds and so they are not completely black. But they are still cold.

Ships are turned to regulate heating and cooling. By turning, a part is alternately heated and cooled; temperature can be kept fairly even. Excessive heating is usually more of a problem than is cooling. In fact, vehicles such as the shuttle orbiter must have radiation panels for getting rid of heat. They are located on the underside of the cargo doors. In flight, the doors are swung open, exposing the panels. Heated water circulating through them picks up heat from the interior and releases it into space.

3 TIME IN OUTER SPACE

What is time?

Time itself is a mystery. Look up the word in a dictionary and you'll find a long and not very clear discussion of what it is. Time is difficult to explain. You might think of it as the interval between two successive events. For example, a solar day is the interval from noon to noon, or from one appearance of the Sun on your meridian to its next appearance. (Your meridian is an imaginary line that passes overhead and extends from pole to pole.)

Most of us measure time in more personal events, such as going to school, getting home, having meals, going to bed, and getting up. If we're having lunch, we know it is around noontime; if we are going to school, we know it is around eight in the morning. We also tell time by sky conditions. If the Sun is rising, we know it is morning; should the sky be dark, we know it is night. A darkening sky usually means sunset and evening.

Our lives become regulated by cycles of events. There gets to be a rhythm to these cycles; our bodies adjust to them by changes in activity.

Although there are a good many "night people," most of us

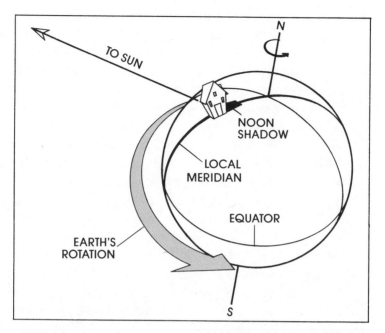

Noon occurs when the Sun is on your meridian. It is the time when shadows are shortest. The interval until the Sun reappears on the meridian is a solar day. It is about 24 hours, the rotation period of Earth.

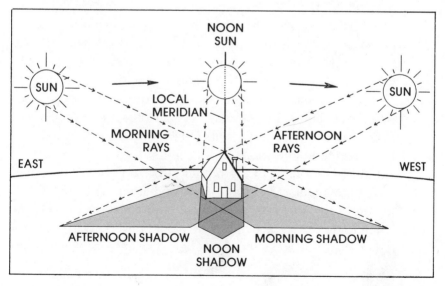

are more active in daylight hours; we are accustomed to the day/night cycle. We get used to going to bed at a certain hour, and as that hour approaches, our bodies get ready for sleep. We have adjusted to a 24-hour cycle, one that is determined by the time it takes Earth to rotate.

Our clocks are built to keep that cycle—two 12-hour periods—or, as with some clocks, one period of 24 hours.

If Earth took only 10 hours to rotate, chances are that people would have adjusted to a 10-hour cycle. Our body rhythms would then be quite different from what they are now.

How is time kept in space?

If you were to spend some time on Mars, you would have no trouble adjusting to its time period. The planet rotates in 24 hours, 31 minutes, so your body rhythms would be maintained just about as they are on Earth.

Should you vacation on the Moon, however, the day/night cycle would be quite different. A day there is about thirty Earth-days long, so there would be two weeks of continuous daylight followed by the same period of continuous night. You would have to establish some other recurring event that would be more in step with your body rhythms. This would also be true at most other locations in the solar system—the day/night cycle is only a few hours on Jupiter, while it is several months on Mercury. And it is true in the shuttle orbiter and in the Russian space laboratory that has been in orbit for several years. When space colonies are built, they will also have to set up their own time intervals.

On the Moon, as in the orbiter, a person's activities would have to be regulated in some artificial manner. There would be a time to get up, have meals, work, rest, relax, sleep. To know when to do various activities, one would have to watch a clock rather than the Sun's location, the occurrence of sunrise and sunset, or the appearance of bright skies and darkness. The clock would be set for 24 hours, as it is on Earth, so the astronauts would keep the same rhythm.

How would time be regulated in space colonies?

If you were to spend a lifetime in space aboard a space colony, some other arrangement would probably be needed. If one were continually surrounded by the same amount of light, the effect might be harmful. Imagine, if you can, that there was no night, no temperature changes, no rain or snow; each morning was exactly the same, and when you went to bed, the brightness was just as it had appeared when you awoke. That would be boring, and far from stimulating. Many scientists believe it would also be disastrous, for people would lose enthusiasm and become less and less active. (Here on Earth those living in higher latitudes experience some of these problems during the long Arctic nights and days which extend over several weeks. Fortunately, the condition seldom becomes unbearable because people know that changes will occur eventually.)

Space colonies will be constructed so that light inside them will be controlled in some fashion. For example, there may be large mirrors outside the colony that direct sunlight evenly to the installation. Blinds mounted above the residents in what amounts to their sky would regulate the amount of light entering the colony. These would be operated automatically by a mechanism controlled by a 24-hour clock. The light could be fully on, as at midday, and gradually decreased toward the evening hours; it would be off during night hours.

This would avoid a good many of the time-adjustment problems that are part of living in space. However, in smaller colonies, sky variations, such as changing colors and the buildup of clouds and rainfall, would not occur. There would be no weather.

Eventually, very large colonies might be constructed. These

In space colonies, light reflected from large mirrors would be controlled to produce a day/night cycle similar to that which exists on Earth. NASA

would be cylinders some 6 kilometers across and 25 kilometers long. They would rotate around the long axis. Transparent sections admitting light would alternate with opaque parts that would prevent light reflected by mirrors from entering the colony. Thus, a day/night cycle would be created. These larger colonies would be of sufficient size for there to be some color in the sky, for clouds to develop, and for rain to fall from them.

Humans have learned how to adjust to all sorts of changes in temperature, pressure, and brightness—a variety of conditions. We can be sure that as space living develops, people will adjust to space conditions, too. Time need not be a problem in those places where environment can be controlled. Earth's 24-hour clock will very likely be the guide.

What is relative time?

In a sense, all time is relative. Something is old only relative to something else that is newer. A clock is fast only relative to clocks that are not fast.

In 1905, Albert Einstein published his special theory of relativity, which concerns space and time. Among other startling statements, the theory said that, relative to a person on Earth, a person in a fast-moving spaceship would not age nearly as much. While years might pass for the Earthbound resident, only hours would go by for the space traveler.

Suppose a ten-year-old boy sets off on a round-trip journey to a distant star. His spaceship, let's say, is going very close to 300 000 kilometers a second—the speed of light. Another boy, the twin of the first, remains on Earth.

After twenty years, the boy on Earth would be thirty years old. Chances are he would be married and have a child or two.

When his space traveling twin returns to Earth, he would not have aged; he would still be ten years old. He would have been gone only 4 hours. He knows this because the clock aboard the ship has registered a 4-hour interval.

This sounds incredible. But it is correct. Time is relative because the speeds governing time for the two boys are relative. One is zero; the other is very nearly 300 000 kilometers a second. Time for the two is different. There is no such thing as universal time; all time is relative.

An argument against travel to the stars is the time needed to make the journey. At ordinary rocket speeds of 100 000 kilometers an hour, journeys to the stars would take centuries. Spaceships of the future may travel much faster, perhaps several million kilometers an hour, and so the journeys would be much shorter.

If ships could be made to go over a billion kilometers an hour, they would be traveling at close to the speed of light. It seems unlikely that this will ever happen. But if it does, Einstein's ideas about relative time could be proved.

A space traveler would age only 4 hours while his counterpart on Earth would age twenty years. Fantastic!

WEIGHTLESSNESS AND ZERO GRAVITY

What is up and down?

Sitting in your chair, you have weight because Earth's gravity is pulling on you. You feel your weight because the chair is pushing up while you are being pulled down. Suppose the room you are in were an elevator. Also, suppose that, suddenly, the elevator dropped at a rapid rate. You would be weightless. If your chair were on a scale, it would register zero.

The elevator would fall down toward the center of Earth. That's the way all things fall on this planet. On Mars, *down* means toward the center of that planet; on the Moon, *down* is toward the center of the Moon.

In space, there is no down. But objects fall. They don't fall down, though, they fall around. The shuttle orbiter falls around Earth. As it falls with its passengers, the astronauts experience the same feeling that you would have if your room were falling as does an elevator. The astronauts are weightless.

There is no up or down for them. The ship itself has mass, so it exerts a pull on other objects. But the force is so small that those inside would not be aware of it. So we say there is zero gravity, although there really is a small amount of gravity. As mentioned in Chapter 1 and explained further in this chapter, gravity never becomes zero.

What is weightlessness?

When a person is weightless, the slightest exertion causes motion. For example, if you pushed yourself away from a chair, you would continue to move away from it. There would be nothing to stop the motion. You would float in space. Should you let go of your book, it would hang in space. Push it ever so slightly, and the book would move in a straight line. Splash water, and it would form into round drops moving in all directions.

Sleeping in space is not as pleasurable as it is on Earth. Part of the comfort of sleeping is snuggling under the covers, feeling your weight on the mattress, and feeling the blanket over you—it holds you in. This is not so in space. Sleeping involves being covered, as on Earth. But to feel secure under the covers, one must be strapped in, since the blankets have no weight and neither do you. Astronauts could sleep in any position because there is no down. However, since they are used to lying down while sleeping, astronauts feel better when they sleep in a position that suggests the beds that are familiar to them.

Outside the orbiter or other spaceships, weightlessness can be a major hazard. Astronauts pushing free of the ship would find that the motion continues. Therefore, astronauts are either tethered to the ship or small jet engines are strapped to them. Since the astronauts cannot walk in space, the only way they can move from place to place is to pull themselves along by using the tether, or by using jet action. The jets cause the astronaut to move in the direction opposite that of the jet. Should the jet fire to the left, the astronaut moves to the right. However, the jets must be fired with precision, since the slightest error would cause the astronaut to go into an uncontrolled spin.

Astronaut Sally K. Ride uses a sleep restraint device at her sleep ▶ *station on the Challenger. This method is just one of several used by shuttle astronauts. Some sleep in various positions with*

either their feet or their upper bodies anchored. NASA

When astronauts go outside the shuttle orbiter, they are usually
tethered to it. They may also wear jet packs that enable them to
move about. Here Astronauts Donald Peterson and F. Story
Musgrave evaluate the Challenger's handrail system.   NASA

How do astronauts adjust to weightlessness?

Our bodies are adjusted to gravity. Our hearts and other muscles work against it, so there is exertion. When a person is weightless, the demands are much smaller, and the muscles become lazy. Astronauts must exercise to keep muscle tone. No one knows how long people can remain in space. However, several have stayed there many months without any long-lasting ill effects.

During the first few hours in space, astronauts usually lose a lot of body fluids. It's because the body reacts to what seems like an excess of fluids. Here on Earth, blood tends to pool in the lower parts of the body; it is pulled down by gravity. In space, there is no pulling down; fluids are spread more evenly throughout the body. There seems to be too much, so fluid-control mechanisms of the body react by causing release of fluids. Salts are expelled with the fluids, including calcium, and astronauts often suffer from calcium deficiency, which causes them to get muscle cramps. In most cases, the effect is easily corrected within a few hours.

What is zero gravity?

Earlier in this chapter, you came across the term zero gravity. Actually, there is no such thing. The force of gravity may drop off rapidly and become very small, but it never reaches zero.

Isaac Newton, the English scientist, discovered centuries ago that two conditions affect the force of gravity between two objects—the masses of the objects and the distance between them. If the masses are increased, gravity is increased. As the distance between the masses becomes greater, the force of gravity becomes less.

Suppose we consider two masses, yours and the mass of the Earth. You exert a pull on Earth, and Earth exerts a pull on you. Your mass is very small, though, so your pull on Earth is insignificant. However, Earth's pull on you can be measured; it is your weight. If you were twice as far from Earth's center, its pull on you would be only ¼ as great; three times farther away, the force would be only ⅑ as great. As distance increased, gravity would drop to ⅟₁₆ of the value at the surface, ⅟₂₅, ⅟₃₆, and so on. The force gets smaller steadily, but it never reaches zero. Gravity of a given mass continues on and on out into space.

As we said in Chapter 1, Earth's gravity is like a well, with steep sides that gradually flare out into a gentle slope. A lot of force is needed to escape from Earth, to climb out of the well. That's why powerful rockets that burn tremendous amounts of fuel are needed to launch ships such as the shuttle orbiter.

You can think of Earth's gravity as a hole, with Earth at the bottom of it. Tremendous energy is needed for a ship to climb out of the gravity well.

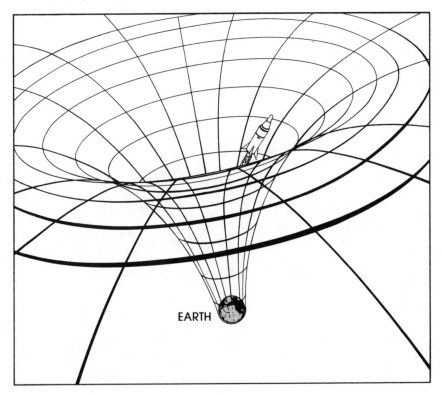

EARTH

Once the shuttle has gained a bit of altitude, it tips slightly and is aimed across the Atlantic Ocean. The next time you watch a launch, notice that the ship starts straight up, but very soon its course starts to curve. The vehicle continues upward, but it curves into a path that will become tangent to Earth's surface. Its height will eventually become fixed at whatever level has been determined for that particular mission, let's say 250 kilometers.

The orbiter is moving forward (coasting) and, at the same time, it is falling. It is in free-fall, and so is everything in it. The situation is like that in the elevator. But everything does not fall to Earth; it falls around the Earth. Its curvature of fall equals the curvature of Earth. The ship is in Earth orbit. Earth's gravity pulls on the orbiter and holds it in orbit. If gravity did not hold it in orbit, the ship would move away from Earth and never return.

How does gravity affect interplanetary flights?

When a probe is sent to Mars, it must be accelerated to high speed, since Earth's gravity well extends out forever. The probe must be pushed strongly at first, but then only a slight push is needed to keep it going. As it gets farther from Earth, the probe slows down. Eventually, it reaches a region where Earth's gravitation has become very low and the gravitational force of Mars becomes a factor.

The probe gets farther into the Martian gravity well. It is pulled into the well, deeper and deeper. Should the probe continue inward, it would go faster and faster and would finally make a crash landing. More likely, the probe would move so that it would go into orbit around the planet, much as the orbiter goes around Earth. Once in orbit, the probe would release a lander that had its own jets. These adjust the speed so, as the lander moves in toward the planet, the gravitation of Mars pulls it in. To prevent a crash, jets aboard the lander slow it down; they work against gravity so the ship can make a soft landing.

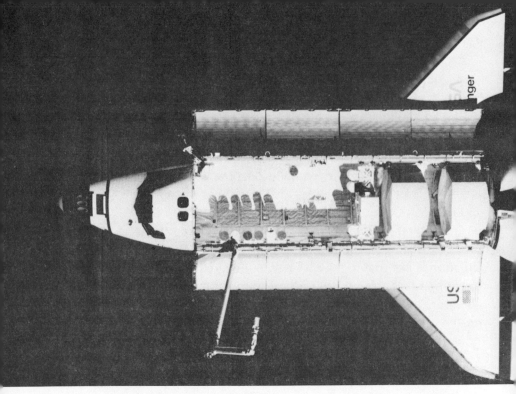

One function of shuttle orbiters is to carry satellites into space. Satellites can be both released and retrieved with the remote manipulator system arm at lower left. NASA

How are flights made from orbiters?

One function of a shuttle is to serve as a launch platform for deep-space rockets and probes. They are carried into space as shuttle cargo. Once the orbiter is in Earth orbit, the hatch doors are opened, and the probe is lifted out. The cargo arm gently places it alongside the orbiter. When the arm lets go, the probe remains in position. Small jets nudge it away from the ship. When it is lined up properly, rockets on the probe fire, putting it into a path that will take it to whatever location has been decided for the mission. It might be to Mars or to some other planet, to an asteroid, or perhaps into an Earth-circling orbit that is some 36 000 kilometers from the surface. That's what was done with the Data and Relay Information satellite launched from the Challenger shuttle in 1983.

Much smaller rockets can launch the probe from an orbiter than would be required for a launch from Earth's surface. That's because the walls of the gravity well are much steeper at the surface than they are out where the orbiter is located.

The shuttle is the antigravity machine of the Space Age. Its huge rocket engines and its boosters fight gravity; they get the ship out of the deepest part of the gravity well. Once in orbit, the orbiter becomes a launching platform that enables deep-space ships and probes to climb farther out of the gravity well. In the future, these vehicles will make long journeys into the gravity wells of distant targets.

With the Earth as a backdrop, a McDonnell Douglas Payload Assist Module (PAM) eases out of the cargo bay of the Challenger, carrying a Canadian communications satellite into orbit. McDONNELL DOUGLAS ASTRONAUTICS COMPANY

5 SURVIVAL IN SPACE

What is needed for survival?

We are Earthbound creatures who flourish because we are adjusted to the conditions that exist here. Our bodies are 70 percent water (the brain is 90 percent water), and so a bountiful supply of water is essential to our survival. Fortunately, water abounds on Earth—in the oceans, the atmosphere, and on the surface.

We live at the bottom of the air ocean that surrounds Earth. The pressure of the air is sufficient to enable our bodies to function properly. At high altitudes, pressure is less. When people go to higher altitudes, they cannot function until certain body changes occur. For example, the number of red cells in the blood increases so that the body can get sufficient oxygen. About 20 percent of the air ocean is oxygen, which is sufficient for our needs. A small amount of the air is carbon dioxide, which is a stimulus to the body's breathing apparatus. Nitrogen, which makes up 80 percent of the atmosphere, provides bulk and volume.

Earth's gravity is another condition to which we have adjusted. It enables us to walk, sit, and move about. It also helps us keep muscle tone, since we must work against gravity constantly. We must lift our feet to walk and use muscles to hold us upright. Even when we're sitting, the muscles are working against gravity. If they weren't, we would collapse.

Adjustment of the body to conditions on Earth has taken millions of years. If the conditions were to change slowly, there would be time for the body to adapt. But should our surroundings change quickly, we could not. When people go into space, they encounter conditions that are different from those here on Earth. Their bodies cannot function properly, so ways must be found to change the conditions.

What is the space environment?

Space is unfriendly to human beings. Just about every condition that exists there is dangerous. There is no air, so a person cannot breathe. There is no pressure, so the body's liquids would boil; they would change to gases, causing the body to expand like a balloon. Temperature is extreme. In sunlight, it is unbearably hot, while it is freezing cold in shadow. There are high energy cosmic particles that could injure anyone exposed to them. Also, a person in space would be bombarded by dust—the particles that produce meteor showers as they move through Earth's atmosphere.

Are cosmic particles dangerous?

In the early moments of the creation of the universe, a good many subatomic particles were left over. They never combined to make atoms. These particles are still flying through space. They contain a lot of energy, so much that, when they strike a surface, powerful X rays are produced. These would be very harmful to a space traveler. Frequent explosions on the Sun also release subatomic particles. These are also capable of causing injury to anyone exposed to them over an extended period.

Neither of these groups of particles bothers us here on Earth. That's because we are surrounded by the atmosphere, which serves as a filter. Chances are good that right now you are being bombarded by cosmic particles. But don't worry. For although high speed particles penetrate the atmosphere, they lose much of their energy as they pass through it, so we are not even aware of them.

What is the solar wind?

Particles ejected during solar explosions make up what is called the solar wind. The particles carry electric charges, so they are attracted by magnetic fields. Therefore, Earth attracts the particles, and so do many of the other planets. The particles tend to form into streams that follow along the magnetic lines of force around the planets. The particles are trapped and held there. During active periods of the Sun, the number of particles increases until they overflow out of the magnetic field and stream into Earth's magnetic polar regions. As the particles move in, they react with atoms in Earth's atmosphere at altitudes of some 100 kilometers, causing impressive displays of the auroras—the northern lights (aurora borealis) and the southern lights (aurora australis).

Anyone going into space must be shielded from particle bombardment. Space suits do this partially, but they are not adequate over long periods. Spaceships are built of more sturdy material and so provide fuller protection. But whether or not even this is enough is still a mystery. The longest anyone has been in space is less than a year. No one knows what might happen should one be exposed for a very long period, as would be the case inside a space colony.

To be on the safe side, space colony plans call for particle shields. They would reflect particles from one surface to another, each surface subtracting some of the energy of the particles. By the time they entered the colony, the particles would be sapped of their energy and so pose no hazard.

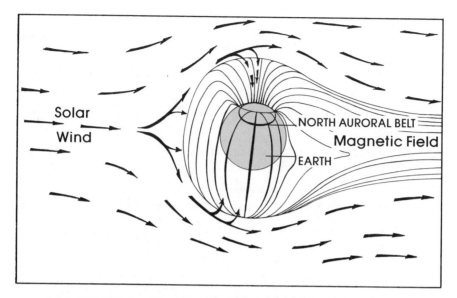

The solar wind, subatomic particles ejected from the Sun, can become trapped in Earth's magnetic field. Occasionally, the particles stream to Earth in the polar regions, stimulating aurora activity.

How can space explorers be protected from meteoroids?

In Chapter 1 we learned that each day some 20 000 tons of meteoroids rain down on Earth. No doubt every shovelful of soil contains meteoroids. Fortunately, they do not affect us because, for the most part, they have little mass. Those that are more massive are usually consumed in the atmosphere. Occasionally a larger meteoroid strikes the Earth, but even then little damage results. Since the 1500s, there have been only about a dozen cases where people have been struck by meteorites—the name given to meteoroids that strike Earth. You wouldn't have to pay much to be insured against loss of life by meteorite bombardment.

Some meteorites are very massive. About a dozen that weigh more than 10 tons have been found. Even though most meteoroids are small and harmless, space travelers must be wary of those occasional larger ones. In space, meteoroids may move some 200 000 kilometers an hour, since there is no atmosphere to slow them down. At such a speed, even small ones might have enough energy to penetrate a space suit or the walls of a spaceship. So far no collisions have been disastrous. But they could be.

Ships designed to remain in space over long periods must have meteor barriers to ward off collisions. Space colonies must also have meteor protection. But even when precautions are taken, a collision might occur. People living in a colony would be drilled in how to handle an accident. If the walls of a colony were punctured, repair crews would rush to the location and patch the break with metal plates stored for the purpose.

Even so, collisions with huge meteoroids might occur, and that could prove to be a major disaster. To avoid such a possibility, instruments scanning space would report the appearance of any massive object. Perhaps the entire colony could be angled to avoid a collision. Or ships might leave the colony to intercept the object. It could be harnessed and made to change course, put into a path that would take it out of the region of the colony.

How is atmosphere produced in space?

In space there is no atmosphere. So there are two problems: There is no oxygen to breathe; and there is no pressure, which is needed for one to breathe properly. In order to survive, people in space must be supplied with both oxygen and pressurized surroundings.

Space suits meet these conditions. They contain a pressurized atmosphere, and the astronauts inside them breathe bottled oxygen. When a person breathes, he gives off carbon dioxide, which is poisonous in large amounts. But space suits are equipped to absorb carbon dioxide, as well as moisture, so the air remains breathable and comfortable. However, the suits are designed to sustain life for only brief periods.

Space shuttles have environment controls that regulate the oxygen supply, the amount of carbon dioxide, moisture, and pressure in the entire cabin. Astronauts do not need space suits while inside the orbiter.

When space colonies are built, they will also have controlled environments. All conditions—such as oxygen, carbon dioxide, water, and air pressure—will be monitored and automatically adjusted to the proper levels. Plants will take in carbon dioxide and release oxygen, and people will take in oxygen and give off carbon dioxide, so a balance should be maintained. If it is not, automatic equipment will add or subtract materials as needed.

What is artificial gravity?

Astronauts and cosmonauts have spent long periods in zero gravity. And, so far as we know, there have been no lasting harmful effects. However, no one knows what might happen to the body of a person if he were born and lived an entire life in zero gravity. But many physicians are concerned. They think our muscles need to work against gravitation, or some similar force, to prevent the muscles from becoming flabby and useless.

People in orbiters experience zero gravity as long as the ship is in orbit. They remain in space for only short periods though, so no problems are anticipated. In a space colony, exposure would be for a lifetime. Very likely, a life of floating free would not be desirable. So colonies are designed to provide artificial gravity, a force produced by motion rather than by mass.

One design is wheel-shaped. Several spokes project from the wheel of the colony to a central hub where ships would dock. The entire wheel spins around the central hub, making a complete turn in one minute. That is slow enough so people inside

A wheel-shaped space colony would turn, producing artificial gravity. For people in such a colony, down *would be toward the outside of the wheel,* up *would be toward the hub.* NASA

will not notice the motion. But it is fast enough to produce a force much the same as that of gravity at the surface of the Earth. It does this by throwing everything away from the hub. When people are standing erect, their heads will be toward the hub, and their feet will push down on the floor, or the ground, which will be toward the outer portion of the tire of the wheel.

Spaceships may eventually set out on journeys that may last for centuries. Such ships will probably be designed to spin in order to create the effect of gravity. One idea is for the ships to be built in two separate sections, each fastened to the end of a long cable. Jets aboard the sections would start the ships turning around one another. Once in motion, they would spin forever since there would be no force to stop them.

Since 1957, when the Space Age began with the launching of Sputnik, engineers have probed a good many of the mysteries of space conditions. We have discussed a few of them. As exploration continues out beyond Earth, new mysteries will develop. No matter what they may be, solutions to them will need to be worked out so that exploration may continue.

 USES OF SPACE

How does zero gravity affect mixtures?

The space shuttle and the Russian space station are leading the way toward further applications. Many of them depend upon zero gravity, which makes possible the production of new metal alloys and mixtures.

Here on Earth, gravity always works on mixtures, tending to separate them. If you were to shake some soil in a jar of water and then set the jar aside, the soil would soon be deposited in layers, with the more massive soil particles at the bottom. That's because gravitation on them is greater than the force on the less massive particles.

In space, the jar of soil and water would remain mixed. There would be no separation, for no gravity would be acting on the particles—all would be in free fall. This property can be used in making all kinds of mixtures that would be uniform through-out. Also, it enables mixtures of materials of different densities to be made and to remain combined. For instance, alloys of steel and magnesium, or of most any other metals, could be made. Such alloys would be much lighter than steel, and it is believed they would be much stronger.

What is a crystal farm?

Crystals are another product that will probably be produced in space. If you look closely at some grains of salt, you'll see that they are actually crystals. A good many substances crystallize once they have been made into liquids. Some of these crystals make valuable gem stones. Others, such as quartz, are used to carry and control electric circuits. Crystal farms in space colonies could produce products that would enable the most positive and unchanging control of electric circuits. This is very important in the development of medical regulating devices, as well as in several types of microcomputers.

In order to have perfect and precise control, the crystals themselves must be perfect. They are difficult to produce on Earth because of pollution picked up from the container, and because of gravity. The solution that is to be crystallized must be pure, but even then, the effects of gravity on it cannot be avoided. In space, purity is no problem, for materials can be liquefied outside of containers. Since containers float free in space, so do liquids. To heat a liquid suspended in space, solar energy can be concentrated so there are no combustion products—such as oxides of sulfur, carbon and nitrogen. Once it is liquefied, a substance can be set aside to crystallize, and the crystals will be absolutely pure and uniform.

What are power satellites?

We are all aware of the rapidly increasing costs of all kinds of energy and the need to expand our reserves because of the tremendous increase in consumption throughout the world. One way of doing this is by using solar energy. It is being used, but not as widely as some people would recommend.

That is partly because there are many limitations to the use of solar energy. During the night there is no sunshine, and during cloudy weather intensity drops off sharply. Also, the Sun is most intense in tropical areas, but the need for energy is greatest in temperate regions where most people live.

One way of overcoming these two big drawbacks is to place solar collectors in space. Engineers have worked out many details of how this could be done, and they are certain the idea can work. The cost would be very high at first, but once the collectors were in orbit they would cost nothing to operate—sunshine is free. The cost of maintenance would also be low, for there would be no moving parts nor would there be any pollution by-products to dispose of.

A typical power satellite would be an array of thousands of solar cells that would change sunlight into electricity. The panel might be 8 kilometers on a side—one that large could produce enough electricity to supply New York City as well as its surroundings. The collector would be made on Earth. Sections of it would be carried into space aboard shuttles. Once there, the parts would be assembled, possibly by robots.

The solar panel would be far enough from Earth to be in sunlight 24 hours a day. Electricity made in the cells would be channeled into a converter. From there it would be transmitted as microwaves to a large antenna on Earth. Once received, the energy would be modified to match that used in our homes, and would be fed into power systems. We would have solar power without interruption by night, clouds, storms, or anything else. There would be a continuous supply—one that would last a long time, since there would be little wear on the equipment.

Right now it is possible to build and install a power satellite, for we have the knowledge and equipment to do so. However, solar cells are still too expensive to be practical on such a large scale, and it's expensive to put the equipment in orbit and assemble it there. Other sources of energy are much cheaper. But, as supplies dwindle and costs go up, people may find that, in spite of the cost, power satellites hold the answer to one of the major mysteries of modern civilization—where can we get

Eventually, solar power collectors in orbit may trap energy and transmit it to Earth in a continuous stream of microwaves. Earth receivers would then convert the energy, making it usable in our homes and factories. ROCKWELL INTERNATIONAL

enough energy to keep the world going, with its ever-growing needs for industry, commerce, transportation, and heating and cooling?

What is a killer satellite?

On October 4, 1957, when Sputnik was put into orbit, warfare changed. Military people knew that whoever could send up a satellite could also use the launch rocket to send a missile around the world. In the years since then, rockets equipped with nuclear warheads have been built. The rockets are poised in underground silos and carried in submarines that cruise the seas, as well as in airplanes that fly the skies.

Rockets have also launched scores of satellites that are going around the Earth, looking down at the various countries of the world, and photographing them. They are powerful enough to show details as small as a person's hand or the numbers on a car's license plates, even though the cameras are several hundred kilometers above the Earth. They are spy satellites that can disclose troop movements and the buildup of missile bases, as well as the missiles themselves.

At this time, the defense system of our country has four communications satellites, weighing a thousand pounds each, and two backup satellites. The satellites connect twenty-seven command centers around the world. The system is being expanded with twelve more satellites stationed 36 000 kilometers away. The satellites are designed to operate for at least ten years. Additionally, our navy has five 2-ton satellites giving a total of twenty-three channels for communication by voice, teletype, video, and computer.

These and other satellites provide vital information to the military. Thirty seconds after a missile is launched anywhere on Earth, American satellites pick it up. There are three satellites, each 6 meters in diameter, that are sensitive to the heat given off when a rocket is launched. Information is sent to Earth stations that then track the missile. Its position, speed, and direction are known exactly.

We also have two satellites located 96 000 kilometers from Earth that can detect, in seconds, nuclear detonations—no matter where they may occur. Four American satellites scan the oceans and inform our command of the locations of all ships— both our own and those of other nations. Weather satellites in polar orbits scan the Earth, keeping watch on clouds and their movements; sky conditions around the Earth are checked constantly.

A satellite service system, using the space shuttle, that would ▶ *inspect, repair, refurbish, or prepare orbiting spacecraft for return to Earth, is currently being investigated.* LOCKHEED MISSILES

AND SPACE COMPANY

Satellites are also vital to navigation. A ship, tank, or plane must know exactly where it is on the Earth and the exact distances to other locations. By the end of this decade, there will be eighteen navigation satellites in orbit. They will tell pilots and captains precisely where they are, to within 10 meters, and they will be able to measure their speed with an error no greater than 10 centimeters a second.

Because satellites provide valuable information, it is to be expected that enemies would try to find ways to destroy them. And they have. One way is to launch what is called a killer satellite. It would be a bomb in orbit. The killer satellite would maneuver close to its target and then be blown up. As it exploded, pieces of the killer would hit and destroy the target satellite. As protection from these killers, target satellites are being made stronger. They are also being equipped with small rocket engines that will enable them to change course and to avoid the attack.

Laser satellites to attack missiles are also being developed. A laser is a tightly focused, highly energetic beam of light. Energy would be so concentrated that the beam would be powerful enough to vaporize a target. And the beam could not be avoided, for it would travel at the speed of light, so fast no target could escape it.

One weapons system suggests that satellites carrying bombs be put in orbit and left there. These bombs would not be used to destroy satellites. They would be released, on command from Earth, and put into paths that would take them to targets anywhere in the world.

Some military authorities believe that the Russian space station is being developed as a weapons platform—a place to store weapons, and a platform from which they could be launched.

At the same time, the United States is developing its own plans for military uses of space. A large part of the payloads carried by shuttle flights are military. Just what they may be remains secret.

In days long past, people said that whichever country controlled the seas, controlled the world. Those were the days when the British Empire was so powerful, largely because it had an unbeatable fleet of ships.

Today people are saying that whichever country controls space, controls the world. That may be. If so, it is important that every nation agrees that space be used for the betterment of all people.

7 MINING THE ASTEROIDS

How were asteroids discovered?

Asteroid means like a star. The name is a good one, for when seen through a telescope, asteroids appear as dim points of light. They look like faint stars. But, unlike stars, asteroids change position from night to night.

In 1781, toward the close of the eighteenth century, the size of the solar system had been almost doubled by the discovery of Uranus. The planet is almost twice as far from the Sun as Saturn, which people had believed was the outermost planet. The spacing of the planets, the distances between them, had become a popular topic of the day. They appeared to be arranged at distances that fit into a mathematical pattern, except there was a large gap between the orbits of Mars and Jupiter.

Some astronomers of that time believed that there was a planet in the gap. At a meeting held in 1796, astronomers agreed to search the sky for the planet. Guiseppi Piazzi made the first discovery of an object in the gap. On January 1, 1801, he sighted a dim object that was not included on star maps. The next night he saw the object again. It had moved slightly, so Piazzi knew it was not a star. Later it was thought to be a minor planet.

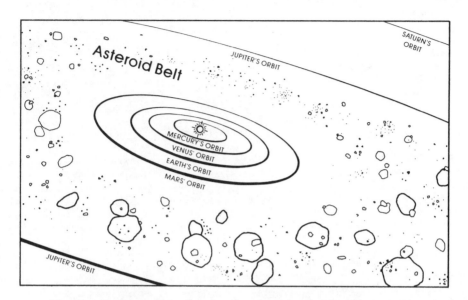

Thousands of asteroids, chunks of rock and metal, move around the Sun in an orbit located between the orbits of Mars and Jupiter. This is known as the asteroid belt.

In reality, it was the first of many asteroids that were to be discovered, most of them in the gap between the orbits of Mars and Jupiter. About sixteen hundred have now been studied. These are the larger ones—from those a few kilometers across to Ceres, the largest, which has a diameter of 765 kilometers. There are probably thousands of smaller asteroids that have not been identified.

What are asteroids made of?

Meteorites, especially larger ones, may have been asteroids that were yanked out of orbit and put on a collision course with Earth. Therefore, by studying meteorites we can learn about asteroids. Ahnighito, a famous meteorite, is on display at the American Museum of Natural History in New York City. It is a chunk of iron and nickel weighing 31 000 kilograms. In 1897, Admiral Robert Peary brought it to New York from Greenland.

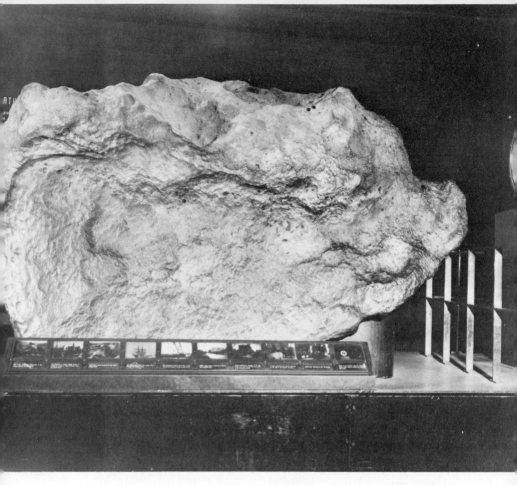

Meteorites such as Ahnighito, which is on display at the American Museum of Natural History in New York City, were originally asteroids. COURTESY DEPARTMENT LIBRARY SERVICES, AMERICAN MUSEUM OF NATURAL HISTORY

Ahnighito is so rich in iron that the Eskimos had fashioned knives and spears from pieces of it and other meteorites found in the same region of Greenland.

Very likely, asteroids are chunks of rock and metal left over from planet formation. They never became consolidated; they never joined together to make a single body. If they had, the objects would not have been very impressive. All the asteroids together would have formed a body no more than 800 kilometers across; you recall that the diameter of Earth is more than 12 000 kilometers.

Lighter materials have escaped from the asteroids, leaving behind the more dense substances, such as iron and nickel. Although all the asteroids together would make only a small planet, even the smaller asteroids contain an impressive amount of valuable raw materials. One only a half kilometer across would contain 400 000 000 tons of pure nickel and iron. In addition, asteroids contain copper, cobalt, and large amounts of stony materials.

Can asteroids be mined?

A medium-size asteroid has enough iron to fill Earth's needs for fifteen years, copper for ten years, nickel for twelve-hundred years, and cobalt for three thousand years. The problem is to get these materials to Earth.

A first step would be to explore for a likely asteroid. It would not be located between Mars and Jupiter, as most asteroids are. This asteroid would be one that had escaped from that region and moved within a few million kilometers of Earth. A manned ship would take off from a space station in Earth orbit. Rockets aboard the ship would fire, placing it in a Sun-circling orbit that would closely follow the orbit of the asteroid. The ship would ease in close to the asteroid and move along with it. Because of its greater mass, the asteroid would pull in the ship and, eventually, the ship would fall toward the asteroid's surface.

The gravitational attraction of the asteroid would be small, just enough to cause the ship to fall gradually to a soft landing. Should the asteroid be more massive, the ship would use braking rockets such as those that eased Apollo landers to the lunar surface.

Astronauts would leave the ship in order to sample the asteroid. After pushing aside dust and loose bits of material, the astronauts would take cores of the crust and analyze the materials contained in it. To learn something of the interior, explosives would be sunk into test holes. The explosives would set up shock waves. From the pattern of the waves, the astronauts could determine density of the materials in the interior of the asteroid. Assuming these proved the presence of iron and nickel, the next step would be to move the asteroid closer to Earth.

This could be done by making the asteroid itself into a rocket. A machine called a mass driver would be constructed. This is a long magnetic accelerator that moves packets of the asteroid's debris to high speeds and ejects them into space. The asteroid moves in the opposite direction. Energy to power the magnets would be obtained from solar collectors erected on the asteroid.

The mass driver would develop only a small amount of thrust. But over a long period of time the effect would be great enough to put the asteroid into a new orbit, one that would move it closer to Earth. As the asteroid came in, the orbit would be modified so that the asteroid would become Earth-circling. It would be parked in Earth orbit.

Once there, bits and pieces of the asteroid would be processed in a space refinery—a plant built in space and powered by the Sun. Earth would be relieved of the tremendous expense, in both fuels and pollution, involved in metal-refining operations. The cost of asteroid mining would be very high, but once operating, the equipment required would last a long time. Refining would be rapid, for the metals are very pure at the start, and returns to the world would be abundant.

Large shuttles, the second generation of those now operating, would carry materials back and forth between Earth and the space station and its connecting refineries.

The mysterious asteroids, the first of which was found on that first night of the nineteenth century, may prove to be the answer to the limited resources of planet Earth. Conservation and wise use—including recycling of the iron, cobalt, copper, and nickel we now have—will extend Earth's supplies. However, a time may come when we shall have to look elsewhere for many of our resources. It's possible that we'll be mining asteroids. Some people believe this could happen early in the next century.

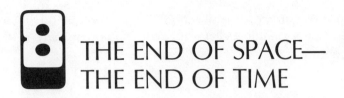

THE END OF SPACE—
THE END OF TIME

Is space moving?

Galaxies are moving away from us, or we're moving away from them. Indeed, wherever one looks, the galaxies show red shifts. Light waves from them are displaced toward the red end of the spectrum. In laboratories, it can be proved that when a light is moving away from an observer, the light becomes redder—the greater the movement, the greater the red shift.

After careful measurements of the red shifts of vast numbers of galaxies, astronomers have discovered that the shift is 50 kilometers per second per megaparsec. (Megaparsec means 1 000 000 parsecs, and a parsec is 3.2 light-years.) This means that the farthest galaxies move the fastest. In a given time period, far-off galaxies move farther than do nearby galaxies.

The galaxies move away from us. And they move away from all other galaxies. We are not the center of the universe. If we could be transferred to some other galaxy, such as Andromeda, all galaxies would appear to be moving away from that one. And so it would always be, no matter what our galactic location might be.

The great galaxy in Andromeda, which some people with espe- ▶
cially good vision are able to see as a dim, fuzzy patch, contains
some 200 billion stars. It is moving away from us—and from
other galaxies.

ALAMAK

M31

Andromeda

MIRACH

ALPHERATZ

MATAR

SCHEAT

Pegasus

MARKAB

ALGENIB

ENIF

HOMAM

BAHAM

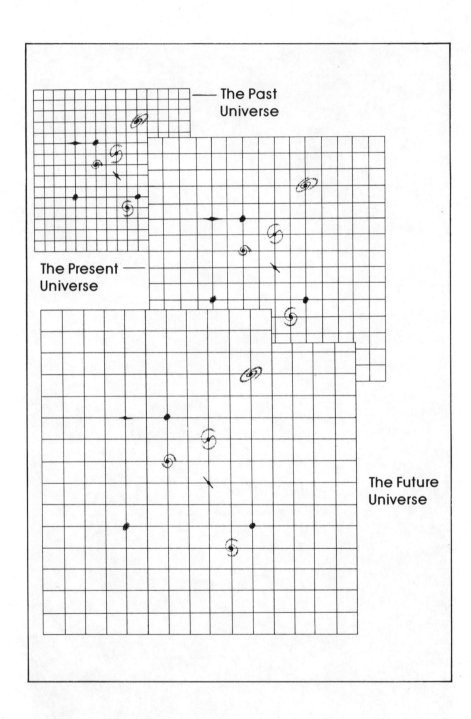

The Past
Universe

The Present —
Universe

The Future
Universe

Is there an end to space?

As distances of galaxies increase, velocity also increases. Another way of saying this: Velocity is an indicator of distance. The fastest-moving galaxies turn out to be 13 to 15 billion light-years away. So that is the size of the presently known universe. But the universe is expanding. Galaxies are not expanding into space. Space itself is expanding, and we know this because we can see that galaxies, which are part of space, are moving farther apart.

All signs indicate that the expansion will continue forever. The motion began with the big bang, a super explosion of a tremendous concentration of the matter of the universe that occurred some 15 billion years ago. The movement of matter started then. It has continued through aeons of time because there has been no force to stop it. And it will continue into the future for the same reason. The only force that could stop the motion is gravitation. So far as can be determined, there is not enough mass in the universe to produce sufficient gravitation to stop the motion and pull the universe together. So it will expand forever.

That means there is no end to space. It also means there is no end to time. Time zero was the moment just before the big bang. Since then, 13 to 15 billion years have elapsed. And time will continue, just as long as the universe continues to expand.

These are conclusions astronomers have reached because of the observations they have been able to make. No doubt as space is explored, new and unimagined mysteries will appear, and they will be investigated. We can be sure that, so long as people are curious, they will continue to be challenged to understand the universe of space and the masses of material that move through it.

◄ *All observations indicate that the universe is expanding—the more distant galaxies are moving the fastest.*

The manned space platform in this artist's rendering is based on the concept of evolution and expansion from an original orbiting power satellite. A habitable unit could be attached, enabling scientists to remain in orbit for several weeks. McDONNELL DOUGLAS ASTRONAUTICS COMPANY

FURTHER READING

Branley, Franklyn M. *Comets, Meteoroids and Asteroids.* New York: Thomas Y. Crowell, 1974.

————. *Mysteries of the Universe.* New York: Lodestar Books, 1984.

————. *Space Colony: Frontier of the 21st Century.* New York: Lodestar Books, 1982.

Heppenheimer, T. A. *Colonies in Space.* New York: Holt, Rinehart and Winston, 1976.

Weiss, Malcolm E. *Far Out Factories: Manufacturing in Space.* New York: Lodestar Books, 1984.

INDEX

Page numbers in *italics* refer to captions.

ABOUT THE AUTHOR

FRANKLYN M. BRANLEY is the popular author of more than one hundred books for young people on astronomy and other sciences, including *Mysteries of the Universe,* the first book in the Mysteries of the Universe series; *Halley: Comet 1986; Space Colony;* and *Jupiter.*

 Dr. Branley is Astronomer Emeritus and former chairman of The American Museum–Hayden Planetarium. He and his wife live in Sag Harbor, New York.

ABOUT THE ILLUSTRATOR

SALLY J. BENSUSEN, illustrator of *Halley: Comet 1986,* has done work for the Smithsonian as well as for many astronomy magazines. She lives in Lanham, Maryland.